You Scratch My Back...

Buffy Silverman

Raintree

Chicago, Illinois

Designed by Philippa Jenkins and Q2A Creative

Printed and bound in China by Leo Paper Group

12 11 10 09 08
10 9 8 7 6 5 4 3 2 1

Library of Congress Cataloging-in-Publication Data
Silverman, Buffy
  You scratch my back / Buffy Silverman.
    p. cm.
  Includes bibliographical references and index.
  ISBN-13: 978-1-4109-2844-3 (library binding -
  hardcover) -- ISBN
  ISBN-10: 1-4109-2844-6 (library binding -
  hardcover)
  ISBN-13: 978-1-4109-2861-0 (pbk.)
  ISBN-10: 1-4109-2861-6 (pbk.)
  1. Symbiosis--Juvenile literature. I. Title.
  QH548.S554 2007
  591.7'85--dc22
                                    2007003286

Acknowledgments
The author and publisher are grateful to the
following for permission to reproduce copyright
material: Corbis pp. **8–9** (George D. Lepp), **26–27**
(Wolfgang Kaehler); FLPA/Minden Pictures pp.
10–11 (Frans Lanting), **14** (Richard Du Toit), **20–21**
(Mark Moffett), **24–25** (Sumio Harada), **28 bottom**
(Norbert Wu); FLPA p. **22–23** (Nigel Cattlin);
naturepl.com p. **13** (Doug Perrine), **17** (Brandon
Cole); Photolibrary/Animals Animals/Earth Scenes
p. **28 top**; Photolibrary/Index Stock Imagery p. **29**;
Science Photo Library pp. **6–7** (Eye of Science), **7**
(Michael Abbey), **18–19** (Edward Kinsman); Warren
Photographic p. **4–5**.

Cover photograph of yellow- and red-billed
oxpeckers on Burchell's zebra reproduced with
permission of Getty Images/Taxi.

Illustrations by Mark Preston.

The publishers would like to thank Nancy Harris and
Harold Pratt for their assistance in the preparation of
this book.

Every effort has been made to contact copyright
holders of any material reproduced in this book. Any
omissions will be rectified in subsequent printings if
notice is given to the publishers.

Disclaimer
All the Internet addresses (URLs) given in this book
were valid at the time of going to press. However,
due to the dynamic nature of the Internet, some
addresses may have changed, or sites may have
changed or ceased to exist since publication. While
the author and publishers regret any inconvenience
this may cause readers, no responsibility for any
such changes can be accepted by either the author or
the publishers.

It is recommended that adults supervise children on
the Internet.

Contents

Some words are printed in bold, **like this**. You can find out what they mean on page 30. You can also look in the box at the bottom of the page where they first appear.

You Scratch My Back

Imagine wading into an African river. A crocodile is near. Would you run away or hide?

An Egyptian plover does not fly away. This bird jumps on a crocodile's back. Sometimes it hops into a crocodile's mouth!

A crocodile's mouth is a good place to find food. Food gets stuck between a crocodile's teeth. The crocodile opens its mouth wide.

The plover hops in. It finds scraps of meat. It pecks at bugs. Bugs crawl on the crocodile's skin. The plover helps the crocodile. It cleans the crocodile's teeth and skin. The crocodile does not try to eat the bird.

Would you look for a meal in a crocodile's mouth?

benefit get something that helps you

symbiosis partnership between different kinds of living

Different kinds of living things can be partners. They **benefit** from living together. One partner may get food or shelter. One partner may protect the other. A partnership between animals is called **symbiosis**. Symbiosis means living together in a special way. One or both partners get something from the relationship.

Egyptian plover

Teamwork

Termites are insects. They chew wood. They live in large nests. The nests have many tunnels. Worker termites crawl through tunnels. They find food for all the termites.

Worker termites cannot **digest** (break down) wood fibers. They rely on tiny living things called **protozoa**. Protozoa live inside the termites' guts. Protozoa can eat tough fibers.

Termites need protozoa. Protozoa help them digest their food. Protozoa also need termites. Termites feed them. Termites give protozoa a place to live.

Both termites and protozoa **benefit** from living together. When partners live together, it is called **symbiosis**. Termites and protozoa have a special kind of symbiosis. They both benefit from living together. This is called **mutualism**.

Tiny helpers

Over 500 kinds of **bacteria** live in the human gut. Bacteria are one-celled living things. Some bacteria make you sick. But others keep you healthy.

bacteria   tiny one-celled living things
digest   break down food into smaller pieces
mutualism   partnership in which both animals benefit
protozoa   one-celled living things found in water or soil

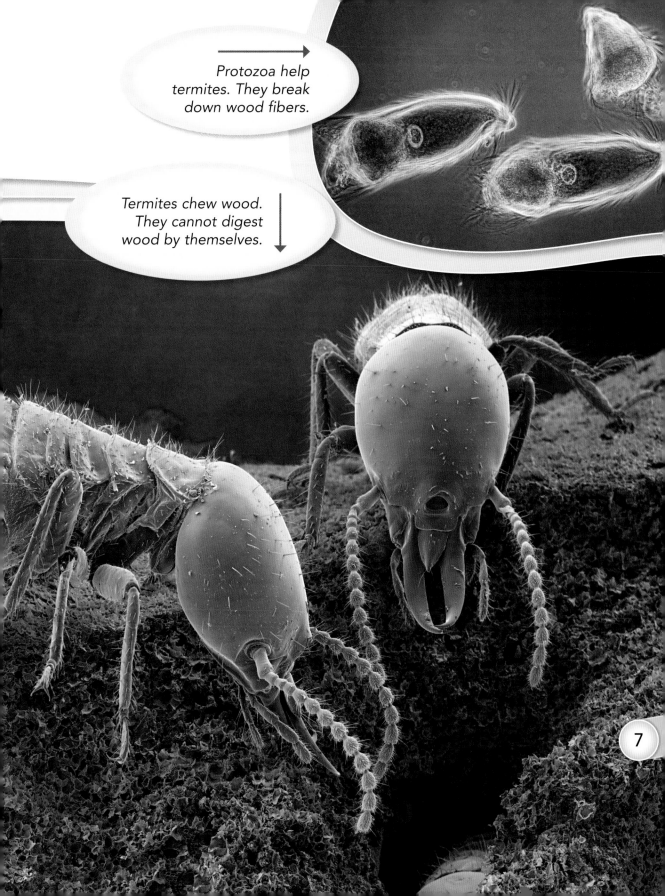

Protozoa help termites. They break down wood fibers.

Termites chew wood. They cannot digest wood by themselves.

A free lunch

A dog scratches. What makes it itch? Fleas! Fleas crawl through the dog's fur. They bite its skin.

Fleas are **parasites**. Parasites feed on other living things. Adult fleas suck an animal's blood. A flea cuts into skin with its mouth. Then, it sucks blood through a tube.

Parasites live on plants and animals. They are called the parasite's **host**. A parasite cannot survive without a host. It gets food from the host. The host carries it from place to place. A parasite may lay eggs on its host.

The host is harmed by parasites. A flea's host gets itchy bites. Sometimes parasites spread diseases when they bite. One partner **benefits**. It gets something that helps it. The other partner is harmed. This type of **symbiosis** (partnership) is called **parasitism**.

A flea can jump up to 200 times its body length. That is like a person jumping 1,200 feet (0.4 kilometers)!

host animal or plant on which a parasite feeds
parasite living thing that lives and feeds on another living thing
parasitism partnership in which one partner benefits and the other is harmed

9

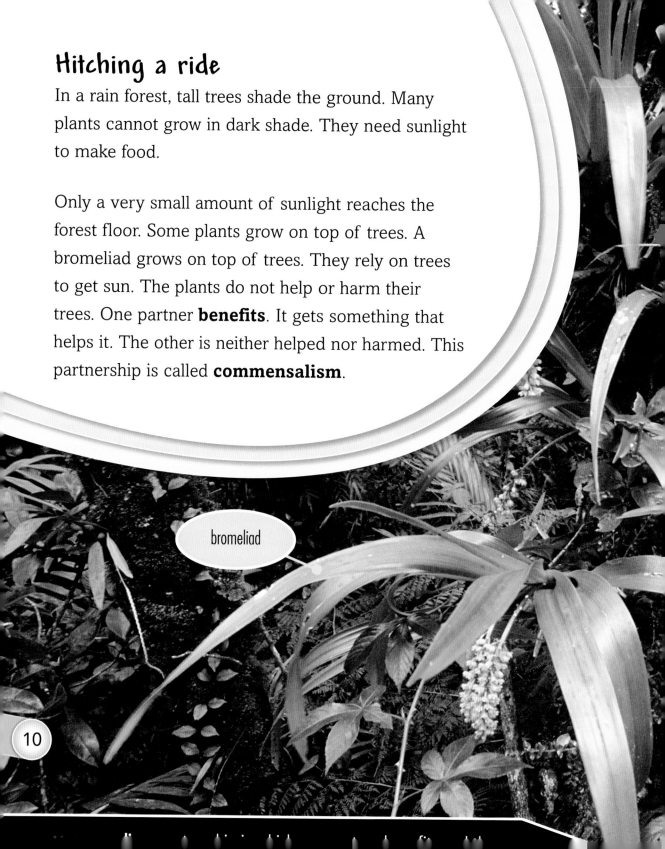

Hitching a ride

In a rain forest, tall trees shade the ground. Many plants cannot grow in dark shade. They need sunlight to make food.

Only a very small amount of sunlight reaches the forest floor. Some plants grow on top of trees. A bromeliad grows on top of trees. They rely on trees to get sun. The plants do not help or harm their trees. One partner **benefits**. It gets something that helps it. The other is neither helped nor harmed. This partnership is called **commensalism**.

bromeliad

Some plants grow on top of trees. Plants get more sunlight by growing on trees.

Animals can also hang onto others to get what they need. Remora fish hitch a ride on sharks. Each fish has a sucker on top of its head. They attach themselves to sharks. Remoras catch food that sharks drop. Remoras benefit from riding on sharks. Sharks are not helped or harmed. This is also commensalism.

Free riders

Some animals live on you! Tiny mites live in human eyebrows and eyelashes. The mites usually do not harm people. They eat oil and dead skin.

Keeping Clean

Would you need a cleaning if you lived in water? Fish do! **Parasites** live and feed on a fish's skin. How do fish get rid of parasites?

Some fish visit a kind of cleaning station. There they find shrimp that eat fish parasites.

Fish living in coral reefs often hunt shrimp. A coral reef is made from the shells of a small creature. The creature is called a coral. Most of the shrimp are dull colored. That helps them hide from fish.

But cleaner shrimp do not need to hide. Fish do not hunt them. Cleaner shrimp are brightly colored. They wave their antennae when fish swim near. They do a special dance.

A grouper fish hovers in place. Cleaner shrimp crawl on the fish. The shrimp eat pests that bother the fish. They even crawl in the fish's mouth. They clean inside it. The fish leaves when it is clean.

Both partners **benefit** from living together. This is **mutualism**. The fish get rid of parasites. The shrimp get a tasty meal.

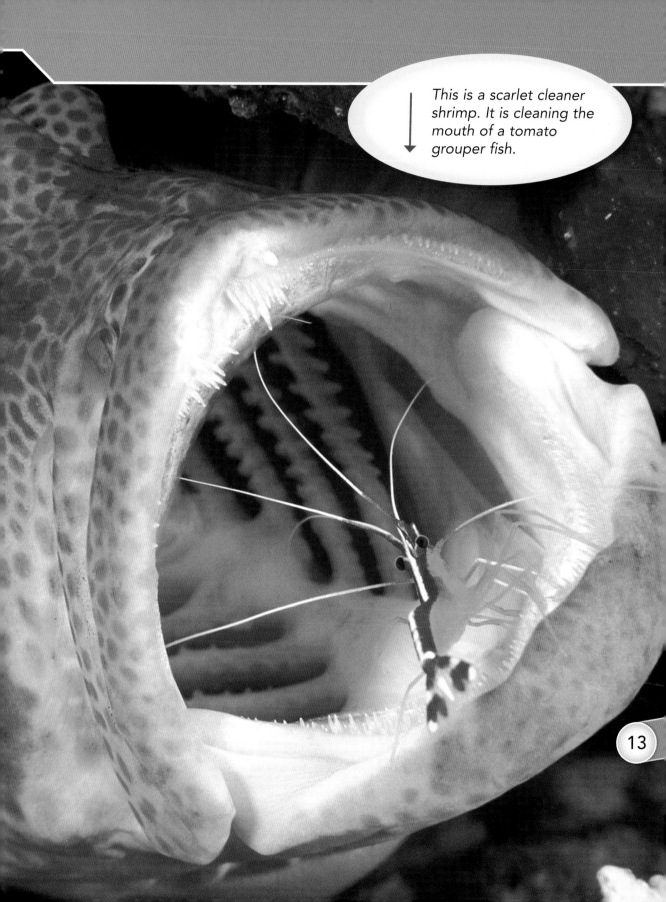

This is a scarlet cleaner shrimp. It is cleaning the mouth of a tomato grouper fish.

↑ Oxpecker birds eat fleas and ticks.

Pest patrol

Oxpecker birds live with zebras. Why does a zebra let a bird perch on its head? The bird cleans the zebra. It pushes its beak into the zebra's fur. It snaps up fleas and other pests.

Fleas and ticks are **parasites**. They live on animals and suck their blood. Parasites can make animals sick. Oxpecker birds eat the parasites off an animal's skin. They keep the animal healthy.

The birds also hiss when they see a **predator**. An animal that hunts another animal is called a predator. A lion is a predator. The hiss warns the zebra to move away.

Both partners **benefit** from living together. Zebras have fewer pests. They are also warned of danger. The birds find plenty of food. This is **mutualism**.

Helpful or harmful?

An oxpecker bird usually helps a zebra. But it can also cause harm. Sometimes an oxpecker does not find ticks. Then it pecks a zebra's ears. It drinks the zebra's blood. It is acting like a parasite!

Staying Safe

Some animals form partnerships to stay safe. One animal protects the other. In return, the animal often gets food.

Sea **anemones** look like plants. But they are animals. Anemones attach themselves to rock or coral. They have long **tentacles** (feelers) with stingers. The tentacles surround their mouths. Anemones wave their tentacles. They sting fish that swim near. Then, they eat the fish.

A boxer crab does not have a stinger. Instead, it holds a pair of anemones in its claws. When a **predator** (hunter) comes near, the crab waves its claws. It looks like a boxer throwing a punch. The predator backs away from the stings. The anemones protect the boxer crab.

What do the anemones gain? Usually anemones stay in one place their entire life. A crab carries anemones on its claws. The anemones catch more food by moving around. When the crab eats, it drops some food. The anemones snag the leftovers. Both partners **benefit**. This is **mutualism**.

anemones

A boxer crab waves anemones in its claws. The anemones keep the crab safe.

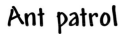

Ant patrol

Some ants care for animals that give them food. Ants care for **aphids**. Aphids are tiny insects that live on plants.

18

aphid	small, soft-bodied insect that sucks sap
honeydew	sugar water made by aphids
sap	liquid food made by a plant

Aphids suck **sap** (liquid food) from plant stems and roots. They do not need all the liquid they drink. Aphids get rid of the extra liquid. It is called **honeydew**. Ants like to eat honeydew.

By caring for aphids, ants make sure they have food. An ant strokes an aphid with its antennae. The aphid releases honeydew.

Ants act as the aphids' bodyguards. Ants crawl up and down stems. They chase away insects that eat aphids. Sometimes there is danger. The ants pick the aphids up. They carry them to safety. Some ants move aphids to new plants with more sap.

Ants and aphids **benefit** by living together. They each get something that helps them. Ants get food. Aphids are protected from **predators** (hunters). This is **mutualism**.

Ants watch over aphids. In return, aphids give ants food.

Animal and plant teams

Some ants care for **acacia** bushes. In return, acacias give them food and a place to live.

How can ants care for a bush? They chase away animals that like to eat the leaves. Ants live in hollow thorns on acacia bushes. They rush out of their thorns when an animal is near. They sting the animal on its nose. The ants also release a scent. The smell warns others to stay away. People and animals avoid acacias with stinging ants.

Ants care for acacias in other ways, too. They move seeds that fall near the bush. That keeps other plants from growing. The acacia then gets plenty of sunlight. This is because no other plants grow nearby.

What do the ants get in return? They live in the bush's thorns. The bush makes sweet **nectar** (liquid). The ants drink the nectar. The ants find all the food they need. Both partners **benefit** in this **mutualism**. They get something that helps them.

thorn

Ants live inside an acacia thorn. They chase away animals that eat acacia leaves.

Pollen Partners

To make seeds, flowering plants need **pollen**. Pollen is a powdery material. It is made by the male part of a flower. Pollen must come from another plant of the same **species** (type). The pollen joins a tiny egg from the female part of the flower. That makes a seed.

Some pollen blows in the wind. But most plants depend on animals to deliver pollen. Plants attract animals with food. Flowers make sweet **nectar** (liquid) for animals. Flowers also make a lot of extra pollen. Animals eat some of the pollen.

Petals attract insects

Pollen is made in the male part of flower

Pollen joins the egg that produces the seeds

Different parts of a flower are used to make new flowers.

pollen   powdery material made by the male part of a flower
species   kind of living thing

Finding flowers

Different colors attract different animals. For example, hummingbirds see red most easily. This means that hummingbirds fly to red flowers.

A bee drinks nectar at a flower. Pollen sticks to her fuzzy body.

Animals do not know that they are helping flowers. They visit flowers to find food. The pollen sticks to their bodies. Pollen rubs off on other flowers when they search for more food.

Stinky flowers

Not all flowers smell sweet. Skunk cabbage flowers stink! They smell like rotten meat.

Flies lay their eggs in warm, rotting meat. If a fly smells skunk cabbage, it thinks the cabbage is rotting meat. So, it flies to the skunk cabbage flower.

Skunk cabbage flowers also give off heat. Skunk cabbage blooms in spring. Snow sometimes covers the plants. The flowers' heat can melt ice and snow.

A hood-shape leaf covers the flowers. It might be cold outside. But inside a flower, it can be 70 °F (21 °C). A fly crawls inside the warm flowers. It gets covered with **pollen**. Then, the fly visits another skunk cabbage flower. The pollen rubs onto the flower. Now, the flower can grow seeds.

Flies and insects crawl inside the skunk cabbage flower on cold nights. Insects need warmth to fly. The skunk cabbage warms them. In return, the insects move pollen from flower to flower. Both partners **benefit**. This is **mutualism**.

Skunk cabbage flowers melt away snow. Flies feel the flowers' warmth and smell their stink.

Perfect Partners

Some plants form partnerships with other living things. A lichen is a plant. It is made of two different living things. It is a partnership of algae and fungi. Lichens grow on rocks and tree trunks.

Algae are green plants. They grow in ponds and rivers. But the algae in lichens grow on rocks. How can they do that?

They depend on fungi. Fungi eat dead plants and animals. The fungi keep algae from drying out. The algae get water and **nutrients** from the fungi. Nutrients are things that algae need to grow.

Fungi often grow on dead things. But when fungi live with algae, they do not eat dead things. They get their food from the algae. Algae can make food using sunlight. Algae make food for the fungi.

In lichens the algae and fungi need each other. The algae get protection. They do not dry out. The fungi get food. Lichens grow in places where neither partner could live alone.

Clean-air lovers

Lichens cannot grow where there is dirty air. It is hard to find lichens in cities.

Lichens look like paint splattered on rocks. Fungi and algae live together on rocks.

Who Helps Whom?

The animals on this page live with other living things. They have a kind of partnership. This is called **symbiosis**. What kind of symbiosis is it—**parasitism**, **commensalism**, or **mutualism**?

A. A tick grabs onto a dog's fur. It sucks the dog's blood. Its body swells like a balloon. The tick needs blood to grow eggs. But the dog itches from the tick's bites. What kind of partnership is this?

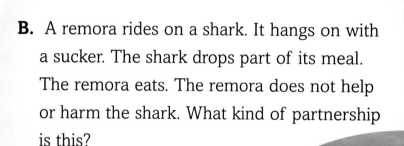

B. A remora rides on a shark. It hangs on with a sucker. The shark drops part of its meal. The remora eats. The remora does not help or harm the shark. What kind of partnership is this?

C. A cow cannot break down grass. **Bacteria** live inside the cow's stomach. The bacteria make special chemicals. The chemicals break down grass fibers. Then, the cow can **digest** grass. The bacteria gets a supply of food. What kind of partnership is this?

Answers:

A. A tick **benefits** from living on a dog. The dog is harmed. This is parasitism.

B. A remora benefits from living with a shark. The shark is not harmed. This is commensalism.

C. The cow and the bacteria both benefit from living together. This is mutualism.

Glossary

acacia bush with thorns. Ants live in thorns on acacia bushes.

anemone sea animal with stinging tentacles. Sea anemones look like plants, but they are animals.

aphid small, soft-bodied insect that sucks sap. Aphids are tiny insects that live on plants.

bacteria tiny one-celled living things. Some bacteria help people break down food, but others cause illness.

benefit get something that helps you. One or both partners benefit in symbiosis.

commensalism partnership in which one partner benefits and the other is not helped or harmed. Plants living high on trees are an example.

digest break down food into smaller pieces. It takes several hours for humans to digest food.

honeydew sugar water made by aphids. Ants drink honeydew.

host animal or plant on which a parasite feeds. A dog is a good host for a biting tick.

mutualism partnership in which both animals benefit. Worker termites and protozoa are an example of mutualism.

nectar sweet liquid made by flowers. Birds feed on the nectar of flowers.

nutrient something that plants need to grow. Plants usually get nutrients from the soil.

parasite living thing that lives and feeds on another living thing. A flea is a parasite.

parasitism partnership in which one partner benefits and the other is harmed. A flea feeding on a dog's blood is an example of parasitism.

pollen powdery material made by the male part of a flower. Plants need pollen to make seeds.

predator animal that hunts another animal. A lion is a fierce predator.

protozoa one-celled living things found in water or soil. Protozoa help termites digest wood.

sap liquid food made by a plant. Aphids suck sap from plants.

species kind of living thing. Humans and dogs are different species.

symbiosis partnership between different kinds of living things in which one or both partners benefit.

tentacle long, bendable feeler. An octopus has tentacles.

Want to Know More?

Books to read

- Aruego, Jose, and Ariane Dewey. *Weird Friends: Unlikely Allies in the Animal Kingdom.* New York: Gulliver, 2002.

- Hirschmann, Kris. *Ticks.* Detroit, MI: KidHaven, 2003.

- Rhodes, Mary Jo, and David Hall. *Partners in the Sea.* New York: Children's Press, 2005.

Website

- http://www.mbgnet.net/bioplants/pollination.html
  Learn more about how pollen is moved from flower to flower.

Read more about how plants and animals live together in ***The War in Your Backyard***.

Find out how some animals get food in ***Shark Snacks***.

Index